Coral ReeFs

Precious McKenzie

ROurke
Educational Media

rourkeeducationalmedia.com

Scan for Related Titles and Teacher Resources

www.rourkeeducationalmedia.com

PHOTO CREDITS: Cover: © Brandelet; Title Page: © Krishnacreations; Page 4: © Jason Register; Page 5, 14: © Richard Carey; Page 6: www.lotsofpixels.com, © Amyydh; Page 7, 11, 14: © Michael Ludwig; Page 8: © Paweł Borówka; Page 9 © Peter Leahy; Page 10: © Cecilia Lim, © Micheal Ludwig; Page 12: © Tetyana Kochneva; Page 13: © Mark Doherty; Page 17: © Vladimir Ovchinnikov, © KJA, © Mark A. Wilson; Page 18: © Zafer Kizilkaya, © Stephankerkhofs, © Jamiegodson; Page 19: © Cs333; Page 21: © NaluPhoto

Edited by Kelli L. Hicks

Cover Design by Nicola Stratford www.bdpublishing.com
Interior Design by Renee Brady

Library of Congress Cataloging-in-Publication Data

McKenzie, Precious, 1975-
 Coral reefs / Precious McKenzie.
   p. cm. -- (Eye to eye with endangered habitats)
 Includes bibliographical references and index.
 ISBN 978-1-61590-313-9 (Hard Cover) (alk. paper)
 ISBN 978-1-61590-552-2 (Soft Cover)
 1. Coral reef ecology--Juvenile literature. 2. Coral reefs and islands--Juvenile literature. I. Title.
 QH541.5.C7M3445 2010
 578.77'89--dc22
                        2010009856

Rourke Educational Media
Printed in the United States of America,
North Mankato, Minnesota

Also Available as:

Educational Media

rourkeeducationalmedia.com

customerservice@rourkeeducationalmedia.com • PO Box 643328 Vero Beach, Florida 32964

Table of Contents

The Most Threatened Place on Earth

Did you know that coral reefs are some of the most threatened habitats in the entire world?

Scientists and conservationists are working to preserve coral reefs because coral reefs are home to 25 percent of the world's **marine** life.

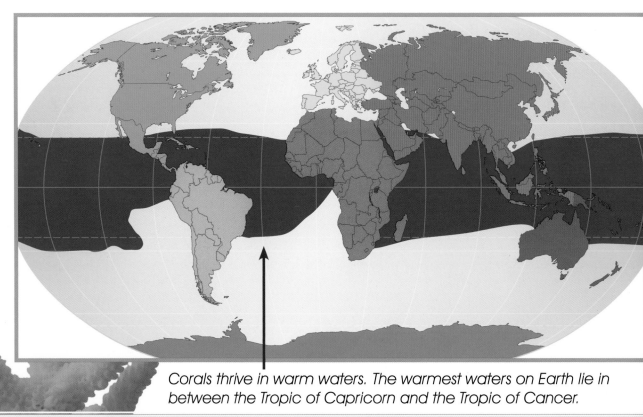

Corals thrive in warm waters. The warmest waters on Earth lie in between the Tropic of Capricorn and the Tropic of Cancer.

Reef Building

Coral reefs are large underwater structures made of limestone, corals, **algae**, sponges, and seaweed.

The main component of a coral reef is the coral itself. But, what is coral? Is it a plant, a rock, or an animal?

Corals are small, soft-bodied animals. Scientists classify corals as relatives of jellyfish and **anemones**.

Translucent jellyfish have tentacles that can sting people.

Sea anemones often house small creatures such as clownfish.

Even though you can not see any fish, it doesn't mean → they are not there. Many fish hide in the coral reef.

Mysterious Polyps

A single coral, known as a coral **polyp**, attaches itself to an underwater rock or on the sea floor. Individual coral polyps live in groups called colonies. Over thousands of years, these colonies can form a coral reef.

Bright and colorful yellow polyps look like beautiful underwater flowers.

Polyps of the species Monastrea cavernosa, or star coral, live → in water between 40 and 100 feet (12.1 and 30.4 meters) deep. Star coral is usually found in the Caribbean Sea.

Yum, Dinner

All coral polyps do not look the same. Different **species** of coral come in different sizes, shapes, and colors.

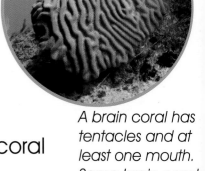

The color of the coral is determined by zooxanthellae algae that live inside the coral. The zooxanthellae provide the coral with **nutrients** so that the coral can thrive.

A brain coral has tentacles and at least one mouth. Some brain coral has more than one mouth!

The top of the coral polyp has tentacles. Coral polyps use their tentacles to catch and then feed on **microscopic** zooplankton which float in the sea water.

Staghorn coral gets its name because it looks like the antlers of a male deer. Staghorn coral grows to almost six feet (two meters) across..

Much like how plants grow, fan coral → attaches itself to mud or sand.

Same Family, So Different

Marine scientists have identified two types of coral. The two types are hard coral and soft coral.

Hard coral secretes limestone. This limestone hardens around the coral polyp like a skeleton. The coral polyp lives inside the limestone skeleton for protection. Hard corals form the **foundation** of coral reefs.

Soft coral is flexible and moves with the waves. Soft coral looks like tree branches blowing in the wind, only underwater!

This hard coral reef in the Red Sea took thousands of years to form, and even though the coral has hardened, more coral will grow on and around the old coral.

12

Scientists recently discovered that the carnation coral, Dendronephythya hemprichi, *feed off of phytoplankton.*

Some Like it Warm

Coral reefs form in clear, shallow water because coral and algae need sunlight to grow. Coral grows best in warm, tropical saltwater. Marine biologists discovered that coral thrives if the water temperature stays between 68 and 90 degrees Fahrenheit (20 and 32 degrees Celsius).

Lionfish, dangerous because of the venom in their fins, call the coral reef home.

Fan coral, like this one, are easily found off the waters of the United States. This one lives near Pompano Beach, Florida.

Reefs of the World

Coral forms three types of reefs. The largest type of reef, a barrier reef, forms near coastlines. Very large lagoons separate the barrier reef from the coastline.

The second type of reef, a fringing reef, forms near coastlines; however, fringing reefs have narrow, shallow lagoons.

The third type of reef, an atoll, occurs when circular-shaped islands of coral enclose a lagoon. The Pacific Ocean is home to most of the world's atolls.

*Geologists determined that it takes at least →
50,000 years for a coral reef to form.*

16

The barrier reefs make ideal homes for young fish and animals because it protects these creatures from powerful ocean waves.

Scientists think fringing reefs are the youngest of all reef types because they grow near the shore. The coral on fringing reefs grow in shallow water and thrive on sunlight.

Atolls are the oldest type of reef taking an estimated 20 to 30 million years to form.

Bustling Reef Life

Many marine animals live in the beautiful coral reefs. Parrotfish, clownfish, jellyfish, starfish, grouper, crabs, shrimp, lobsters, turtles, eels, clams, rays, and octopi are just a few of the interesting creatures who call coral reefs home.

Clownfish act aggressively toward other creatures when they come near their home.

Giant clams eat zooplankton and phytopiankton and can weigh up to 500 pounds (227 kilograms).

Parrotfish love the algae that grow on the reef and use their teeth to grind up the coral!

The octopus is one of the largest predators in the coral reef → habitat, preying upon crabs, scallops, snails, and sometimes fish.

Handle With Care

The coral reef **ecosystem** is extremely **fragile**. Reefs face many threats. Perhaps the most immediate threat is climate change. With climate change comes rising water temperatures. Very warm water hurts coral reefs, slowing down the growth of coral.

Pollution is another threat to coral reefs. Human sewage, run-off from pesticides and fertilizers, poison coral reefs. Offshore drilling and gas pipelines harm the physical structure of reefs. Overfishing threatens the delicate balance of food resources available for the animals in coral reefs.

Dead or dying coral loses →
its beautiful, vibrant colors.

How You Can Help

There are many simple ways you can help protect coral reefs. Since most household cleaning products and lawn chemicals end up in our waterways, use natural, biodegradable cleaning products and detergents that won't poison coral reefs.

Do not give coral as gifts and choose your aquarium fish wisely. Ask store owners where the aquarium fish came from. Only purchase legally **harvested** aquarium fish.

If you live near a shoreline, volunteer in a beach clean up event.

Pick up your own trash and if you see trash on the shore, pick it up, too. This will prevent trash from drifting out to sea.

Please recycle! Recycling reduces the amount of waste in landfills and prevents toxic runoff from flowing into our waterways.

Doing these little things make a tremendous difference in preserving the world's amazing coral reefs.

Glossary

algae (AL-jee): small plants that do not have roots or stems and grow in water

anemones (uh-NEM-uh-neez): marine polyps that look like flowers, but have tentacles

ecosystem (EE-koh-siss-tuhm): a community of plants and animals

foundation (foun-DAY-shuhn): the base on which something is built

fragile (FRAJ-il): very delicate and easily broken

harvested (HAR-vist-id): collected

marine (muh-REEN): to do with the sea

microscopic (mye-kruh-SKOP-ik): very small, unable to be seen without using a microscope

nutrients (NOO-tree-uhnts): vitamins, minerals, and proteins needed to stay alive

polyp (POL-ip): a small sea creature with a tubular body and tentacles

species (SPEE-sheez): a group of animals or plants that have the same characteristics

Index

Websites to Visit

www.kids.nationalgeographic.com/Photos/Coral-reef
www.liveblueinitiative.org/
www.defenders.org/wildlife_and_habitat/habitat/coral_reef.php

About the Author

Precious McKenzie was born in Ohio, but has spent most of her life in south Florida. Her love of children and literature led her to earn degrees in education and English from the University of South Florida. She currently lives in Florida with her husband and three children. They try to do their part by recycling.

Meet The Author!
www.meetREMauthors.com

24